Wish You Were Here

Fourteen Poems about Holidays

ex libris

Candlestick Press

Published by:
Candlestick Press,
Diversity House, 72 Nottingham Road, Arnold, Nottingham NG5 6LF
www.candlestickpress.co.uk

Design and typesetting by Craig Twigg

Printed by Bayliss Printing Company Ltd of Worksop, UK

Cover illustration © Lana Brow/Shutterstock

Candlestick Press monogram © Barbara Shaw, 2008

© Candlestick Press, 2024

ISBN 978 1 913627 41 6

Acknowledgements

Thanks are due to the authors listed below for kind permission to use their poem, all of which are published here for the first time:

Carole Bromley, Jeanette Burton, LB Jørgensen, Beth McDonough, Claire Lynn, Stephen Payne, Pete Taylor, Polly Walshe and Sarah Ziman.

The other poems in this pamphlet are reprinted from the following books, all by permission of the publishers listed unless stated otherwise. Every effort has been made to trace the copyright holders of the poems published in this book. The editor and publisher apologise if any material has been included without permission, or without the appropriate acknowledgement, and would be glad to be told of anyone who has not been consulted.

Thanks are due to all the copyright holders cited below for their kind permission:

Wendell Berry, *New Collected Poems* (Counterpoint, 2012). Poem copyright ©2012 by Wendell Berry and used with permission of Wendell Berry and the publisher. Richard Blanco, *Looking for the Gulf Motel* (University of Pennsylvania Press 2012) by permission of University Pennsylvania Press. Rita Dove, *Playlist for the Apocalypse: Poems* (WW Norton, 2021). Used by permission of WW Norton & Company, Inc. Steve Waling, *Calling Myself On The Phone* (Smith|Doorstop, 2003). All other poems first published in this pamphlet.

All permissions cleared courtesy of Dr Suzanne Fairless-Aitken –
Swift Permissions swiftpermissions@gmail.com.

Where poets are no longer living, their dates are given.

Contents   **Page**

That Moment

When the car rounds a bend or crests
a hill and you catch the first glimpse, leaning forward
in your seat, shedding the miles, the hours, the years
and you sing the song that lays claim to the sight
I can see the sea, the sea, the sea, I can see the sea
taste the salt on the back of your wrist and though
you can't hear the waves over the noise of the engine
the wind rushing past the windows, you feel the pull
of the tide in your blood, the movement, the endless
restlessness of it, the blue horizon making a space
behind your eyes – you can see the sea and already
you're kicking off your shoes

Claire Lynn

Vacation

I love the hour before takeoff,
that stretch of no time, no home
but the gray vinyl seats linked like
unfolding paper dolls. Soon we shall
be summoned to the gate, soon enough
there'll be the clumsy procedure of row numbers
and perforated stubs—but for now
I can look at these ragtag nuclear families
with their cooing and bickering
or the heeled bachelorette trying
to ignore a baby's wail and the baby's
exhausted mother waiting to be called up early
while the athlete, one monstrous hand
asleep on his duffel bag, listens,
perched like a seal trained for the plunge.
Even the lone executive
who has wandered this far into summer
with his lasered itinerary, briefcase
knocking his knees—even he
has worked for the pleasure of bearing
no more than a scrap of himself
into this hall. He'll dine out, she'll sleep late,
they'll let the sun burn them happy all morning
—a little hope, a little whimsy
before the loudspeaker blurts
and we leap up to become
Flight 828, now boarding at Gate 17.

Rita Dove

Postcard from Athens

I'm eighteen. I'm standing at the Acropolis
with Jane and 'Pooch' and Celia Whitchurch.
I'm wearing that red flowery dress Auntie Joy made
and dark glasses I don't remember buying.
On my feet flip flops. What a climb it was
and the sun so fierce we all bought hats
from the man half way up the hill
though they cost half my V form allowance,
it being 1967, the summer of the Colonels
and tanks on every street corner.
Pooch is in love so we had to find American Express
to pick up letters from her sweetheart.
I know nothing about the Parthenon except
it's somewhere to sit down and the view's great
and round our feet stray cats yowl and beg
and we want to put them in our pockets
and smuggle them into our hotel room.
Last night I wrote my postcards home
and handed them in at reception
with the correct change. He won't post them,
just pinch the money. It's three to a room
and we travelled by train. I get the put-u-up
but I don't care. Tonight, we will go to Daphne
for a wine-tasting and someone will say
The retsina grows on you and I will reply
Yeah, like a fungus. We are so sun-burnt,
our red skin will warm the bus to Cape Sounion
where the sea will be the colour of Quink.
We'll never come back though we say we will
but all our lives we'll remember these pillars,
the scrawny kittens, the colour of the sky.

Carole Bromley

Right now,

I want you to wobble me one of your postcards,
deep-dug in biro, whilst on an overnight train.
I'm expecting you somewhere in darkness
squinting at windows, framed in a *diretto*
stopping too often between Prato and Rome.
Teeter me one of your postcards, crumple-faced,
with a sun-faded black and white photo
of a chestnutted road in Grenoble.
Something you'd picked up and laughed at
from a rattly card rack very near Carcassone.
Your message must shout out in upper case,
tell me how E PERICOLOSO SPORGERSI
or, less controversially nowadays
VIETATO FUMARE. I know.
No need for your name. Just send me signs.

Find me caught between rearranging overdue
routine dental appointments or scrambling for lost
document policy numbers, or captured
by WhatsApp to do asks.
Wobble me one of your postcards. Right now.

Beth McDonough

The Vacation

Once there was a man who filmed his vacation.
He went flying down the river in his boat
with his video camera to his eye, making
a moving picture of the moving river
upon which his sleek boat moved swiftly
toward the end of his vacation. He showed
his vacation to his camera, which pictured it,
preserving it forever: the river, the trees,
the sky, the light, the bow of his rushing boat
behind which he stood with his camera
preserving his vacation even as he was having it
so that after he had had it he would still
have it. It would be there. With a flick
of a switch, there it would be. But he
would not be in it. He would never be in it.

Wendell Berry

Looking for The Gulf Motel

Marco Island, Florida

There should be nothing here I don't remember . . .

The Gulf Motel with mermaid lampposts
and ship's wheel in the lobby should still be
rising out of the sand like a cake decoration.
My brother and I should still be pretending
we don't know our parents, embarrassing us
as they roll the luggage cart past the front desk
loaded with our scruffy suitcases, two-dozen
loaves of Cuban bread, brown bags bulging
with enough mangos to last the entire week,
our espresso pot, the pressure cooker—and
a pork roast reeking garlic through the lobby.
All because we can't afford to eat out, not even
on vacation, only two hours from our home
in Miami, but far enough away to be thrilled
by *whiter* sands on the *west* coast of Florida,
where I should still be for the first time watching
the sun set instead of rise over the ocean.

There should be nothing here I don't remember . . .

My mother should still be in the kitchenette
of The Gulf Motel, her daisy sandals from Kmart
squeaking across the linoleum, still gorgeous
in her teal swimsuit and amber earrings
stirring a pot of *arroz-con-pollo*, adding sprinkles
of onion powder and dollops of tomato sauce.
My father should still be in a terrycloth jacket
smoking, clinking a glass of amber whiskey
in the sunset at The Gulf Motel, watching us
dive into the pool, two boys he'll never see
grow into men who will be proud of him.

There should be nothing here I don't remember . . .

My brother and I should still be playing *Parcheesi,*
my father should still be alive, slow dancing
with my mother on the sliding-glass balcony
of The Gulf Motel. No music, only the waves
keeping time, a song only their minds hear
ten-thousand nights back to their life in Cuba.
My mother's face should still be resting against
his bare chest like the moon resting on the sea,
the stars should still be turning around them.

There should be nothing here I don't remember . . .

My brother should still be thirteen, sneaking
rum in the bathroom, sculpting naked women
from sand. I should still be eight years old
dazzled by seashells and how many seconds
I hold my breath underwater—but I'm not.
I am thirty-eight, driving up Collier Boulevard,
looking for The Gulf Motel, for everything
that should still be, but isn't. I want to blame
the condos, their shadows for ruining the beach
and my past, I want to chase the snowbirds away
with their tacky mansions and yachts, I want
to turn the golf courses back into mangroves,
I want to find The Gulf Motel exactly as it was
and pretend for a moment, nothing lost is lost.

Richard Blanco

a walk with daughters at Merthyr Mawr

across an otherworldly place of cuckoo bees and keen stiletto flies
I set a steady pace – the gift of sound and vision in our ears

the skulking slacks and hollows pink and damp with pimpernel
with purple thyme and wildfire asphodel and common flax

look over there girls – there's a rabbit at the mercy of the scrubland
where so many once ran free before their habitat was lost

where dog rose fights with catnip in among the hardy buckthorn
and the marjoram is seasoned by fritillary and marbled white

just maybe we're a month too late – I fold our handy guide
not having found the advertised eleven kinds of orchid flower

and with the afternoon's electric blue now fading to a tired light
the red-legged choughs fan-tailing off towards Porthcawl

we wander back towards the tented terraces where families flock
above the he/she seascape blue and teal as Bowie's eyes

Pete Taylor

Salobreña

As we walked along the beach on the evening we arrived, our host told us that she sometimes saw dolphins in the bay. Staring out towards Africa, I found it easy to believe: every glint, every cloud-shadow. Soon, even when there were no promising signs, I was able to project a pod of dolphins onto the screen of the Mediterranean and enjoy their exuberance, their darting arcs and flashing splashes. I could tune in to their crazy, laughter-filled conversations over the hush of the surf. Through the week, though they never came, it was easier and easier to see them. Later, in the sunny afternoons and the pink dusks, there were whales too — why not? Tall white spouts would give them away and then often they would breach, hurling their mass into the sweet Andalusian air.

Stephen Payne

My dad orders four drinks at a restaurant on the Greek island of Zakynthos, 1987

When my dad was younger, say, forty years old,
he had a Mediterranean look about him, black hair,
a thick moustache like Costas in *Shirley Valentine*.
How disappointing, then, to hear him speak English
when we travelled abroad for our annual family holiday.
I expected him to have an easiness with the waiters
who I imagined were his long-lost family, brothers even.
But my dad didn't wink like they did, or lean against awnings
like it was an art, or lithely wind his way through tables and chairs,
arms held aloft, balancing four or five dishes on spread fingers.
Instead, he tried to catch our waiter's eye, mouthed the words
Can we order, please? then consulted his Casio wristwatch,
as if we were late for an important meeting back at the hotel.
The waiter slid over, still mid-discussion with the gesticulating chef.
Note pad flipped open, pen at the ready, he moved from Greek
to English: *Yes, what can I get you?* like shifting down a gear,
effortlessly slick as the cats meowing down by our feet.
My dad overenunciated *twooo large coke and twooo large beer*,
spiked four fingers in the air, pointed to a pint glass for size.
The waiter nodded, clicked his pen closed, stuffed the note pad in
his back pocket and disappeared into the darkness of a back room.
I remember the embarrassment, me and my brother drawling out
daaaaaad! but it passed, far too hot to linger on such feelings.
It's only now, years later, I start to wonder. Maybe the waiter
laughed as he gathered together the drinks on a tray, flicked off
the bottle tops, added striped straws and a couple of beer mats.
Maybe, like a drachma tossed into a tip jar, he dropped it casually
into conversation where it was bandied about and soon forgotten.
Or maybe he sat down for a moment in the coolness of that room,
away from the customers, slowly sipped on a hot black coffee,
his mind wandering to his kids playing in the local football game,
his wife adding pearl onions to the simmering pot of beef Stifado.
I want him to sit there for a few minutes more, hours, days even,
thinking to himself, in Greek, *let them wait...let them wait.*

Jeanette Burton

Holiday Rental

There's always something to admire
About the place you pick:

The narrow breakfast bar (more of a broken shelf)
Redeemed by a waterfall of morning light,

That ivied window overlooking
A yard with a broken fountain in it

Or the way the front door splits in half
So you can lean out and graze on passers by

Like the old workhorse you are.
Even the worst houses hold benefits:

Freedom to park at a neglectful slant
As if returning from a chase

Or the discovery that your own home
Is a place you love.

You become a visitor to yourself,
Appearing in the small chipped bathroom glass

Not at all as you expect,
As if this 'I' is a temporary let,

This face no more than a season's interface,
Which makes you wonder who you are,

Where you really live.

Polly Walshe

The Guest Book

It's the fifth morning before they notice it.
Squat as a toad, beneath the open folder
filled with instructions for the immersion heater,

where to leave the recycling bags, find spare bulbs,
and hopes they'd have a pleasant stay. Mock crock
with worn gold lettering, and usually a laugh

to read what Roy and Cheryl most enjoyed,
Jane's gripes about the sofa springs, church bells,
the ancient bath that took too long to fill.

But there it is, in biroed nervous scrawl, those
who had left their thoughts at all – others too
had departed before their week was through,

felt unseen eyes upon their backs, that cold patch
in the so-called snug. A Mrs Broom, of Hull,
recounts her wedding ring, lost two days, until –

following the distant sound of a spinning coin –
it reappeared, silent on the dusty sill
in an unused second room. But that was '94.

These days shelves gleam, and smell like Pledge.
Nonetheless, no names returned for more: not Brooms,
not Smiths, not Wilson-Gores, nor honeymooners Sam and Jack.

It's dawn. They'll breakfast on the road. And after all,
their stuff's all packed. She breathes out as she locks the door.
He starts the car. They don't look back.

Sarah Ziman

Tea House Trekking

Travellers are anonymous in lycra, hiking boots, knitwear
till we meet at tea houses in the mountains
that illustrate the difference a letter can make

lovely changing to lonely and back
and the map grows like a trail of breadcrumbs
we leave each other; chance encounters and conversations

rise like sparks, bright against the sky
under stars whose light has travelled far
but still remembers it used to be fire.

LB Jørgensen

What I did on my Holidays

There was a horse in it. Sheep
penned in by a high iron fence
and a locked refinery gate. Clouds,
where the sky hung its lip at me,
hands in my pockets and peevish
on a headland of great escapes
and winds overacting on the cliffs.

I was in the wrong skin, under canvas
on a wet Bank Holiday, so I trailed
behind the family as we walked
to Heysham and back. The part
of my brain with a horse in it
galloped West over Morecambe Bay
like the Lone Ranger, dodging the
quicksands and arguments as I rode
my own shadow over the cliffs.

Steve Waling

Holidays

The holiest of all holidays are those
  Kept by ourselves in silence and apart;
  The secret anniversaries of the heart,
  When the full river of feeling overflows;—
The happy days unclouded to their close;
  The sudden joys that out of darkness start
  As flames from ashes; swift desires that dart
  Like swallows singing down each wind that blows!
White as the gleam of a receding sail,
  White as a cloud that floats and fades in air,
  White as the whitest lily on a stream,
These tender memories are;— a Fairy Tale
  Of some enchanted land we know not where,
  But lovely as a landscape in a dream.

Henry Wadsworth Longfellow (1807 – 1882)